The Merry Adventures of Robin Hood

Adapted by Sheila Lane and Marion Kemp
from the story by Howard Pyle

Illustrations by Hugh Marshall

Take Part Series

Ward Lock Educational

The Merry Adventures of Robin hood

Adapted by Sheila Lane and Marion Kemp

from the story by Howard Pyle

First published by Dover Publications 1968
This adaptation first published by Penguin
Books 1973
This edition published by Ward Lock
Educational 1975
Reprinted 1988

© Sheila Lane and Marion Kemp 1975

ISBN 0 7062 3487 1

Printed in Hong Kong
for Ward Lock Educational
47 Marylebone Lane, London W1M 6AX
A Ling Kee Company

Contents

List of Characters

Robin Hood

Little John (Stranger)

Will Scarlet

Midge, the Miller's Son

Friar Tuck

The Lord Bishop of Nottingham

The Sheriff of Nottingham

King Richard the Lionheart (An unknown Abbot)

★ *This sign means that you can make the sounds which go with the story*

Chapter 1
Robin hood and the Stranger

Here are the people who take part in Chapter 1:

Robin Hood

Stranger (Little John)

Will Scarlet

Robin Hood is in Sherwood Forest. He is running towards a narrow bridge.★ A stranger is already on the other side.

Robin   Stand back.

Stranger   Not I.

Robin   Stand back, I say.

Stranger   Stand back yourself.

Robin   Stand back and let the better man cross first.

Stranger   I AM the better man, so get back to the other side and let me cross.

Robin   Do you want my arrow in your ribs?

Stranger   Do you want my stick on your back?

Robin   Don't you know that I can send an arrow right through your heart before you can wink an eye?

Stranger   Don't you know that I can tan your hide with my stick till you are all the colours of the rainbow?

Robin   You talk like an ass, stranger.

Stranger   You talk like a coward, stranger.

Robin   By my faith, I am not a coward. No man has ever called me a coward.

Stranger   I call you a coward, because you stand there on the bridge with a bow and arrow in your hand. Look! I have nothing to fight with but my stick.

Robin   You shall not call me a coward. I'll throw away my arrows and cut a stick from the forest to match the one you carry.

Stranger   I'll wait here on my side of the bridge and then we'll fight. Cut a good, strong stick, stranger. You'll need a good, strong one if you are going to fight with me.

Robin   I'll trim this oak tree branch.★ There! Now it's ready.★

Stranger   We'll fight right ON the bridge.

Robin   So you want a drink of water do you, stranger? I'm ready and I'll strike.★

Stranger   I don't call that a strike. Take that!★

Robin   And you take that!★ How now! Where have you gone?★

Stranger   I am right HERE! But watch my blow . . . take that . . .★ and down you go, into the water!★
What are you fishing for, stranger? How are the fish down there?

Robin   Swimming away in fright! Give me your hand and pull me to the bank. My head is buzzing like a swarm of bees.

Stranger   The water will cool it then! But here's my hand.★ By my soul, you fought like a true man, my friend.

Robin   So now you call me friend instead of coward. I have more friends within the forest, stranger. Listen! I'll blow my horn.★

Stranger   Who will come for a hunting horn? I'll not be friends with dogs.

Robin   Those who answer Robin's call don't bark! They make no sound. Look over there, between the trees.

Stranger   By my faith! There must be twenty men, all dressed in green.★

Will Scarlet   Good master, what is this? You're wet right to the skin.

Robin   This stranger tumbled me into the water.

Will Scarlet   I'll call the men. They . . .

Robin   No! Don't move. This giant fought me fair and true. He is my friend.

Will Scarlet   We need more men, good master. Will you have him in the band?

Stranger   Your master's not the man for me to serve. I am the one who won the fight.

Robin   I'll prove myself the better man. We'll have a shooting match and I will prove myself.

Will Scarlet   Well, stranger, what do you say to that?

Stranger   If he can prove a better shot, I'll be his man.

Robin   Set up the target, Will. Take a straight piece of white wood bark. ★Mark it four fingers wide and we'll walk back some four score paces.★

Will Scarlet   The target's set, good master. Who shoots first?

Stranger   I'll take first shot. Now! Stand clear. ★ I'll take my aim. ★ Fair and true! My arrow's there, right in the wood.

Robin   Now let me take your place. The target set was just four fingers wide. Now watch me split your arrow! ★

Stranger   You have! By my faith, you have! You've split my arrow as it stood there in the target.

Will Scarlet   Have you ever seen a shot like that before?

Stranger   In all my life, I've never seen an arrow split in two at four score paces. Who is this man?

Robin   They call me, Robin Hood. And those you see between the trees they call my merry men.

Stranger   The one they call, 'The Outlaw'?

Will Scarlet   This is the man. NOW will you join our band and have this Robin Hood to be your master?

Stranger   With all my heart, I will! Give me your hand, good Robin. John Little is my name.

Robin   I'll blow my horn again. ★ My men must meet the man who ducked their master and still lives!

Will Scarlet   He says his name is John Little, but he is the biggest LITTLE that I did ever see.

Stranger   Well, call me Little John, and take my hand.

Robin   We'll christen Little John in our own way. Bring me a pot of ale.

Stranger   How now! What is this?

Will Scarlet   We name you . . . Little . . . John . . . ★

Robin   . . . by emptying a pot of ale upon your head!

And thus it was that Little John joined Robin Hood's band and became his right-hand man.

Chapter 2
Robin hood and Midge the Miller's Son

Here are the people who take part in Chapter 2:

Robin Hood
Little John
Will Scarlet
Midge, the Miller's Son

Robin Hood, Little John and Will Scarlet are sitting by the roadside finishing their midday meal of bread, cheese and brown ale. ★

Will Scarlet	I'll give my last bit of bread to the birds.
Little John	Pass me the goatskin, Robin, and I'll drain the last drop of brown ale down my throat. ★
Robin	Quick! Leave the ale! Take cover in the trees. ★ There's someone coming down the road. ★
Will Scarlet	He's all in white.
Little John	I do believe it's that young Miller's son from over Nottingham town. His clothes and face are dusted down with flour.

Will Scarlet   He's got a sack across his back. I wish it was a skin of ale.

Robin   Let's play a trick and pretend to rob him of his sack. And then, to make things even, we'll fill his purse with money and feast him in the greenwood.

Will Scarlet   What say you, Little John?

Little John   We've nothing else to do. Let's have some fun.

Robin   Listen! ★ He comes. HOLD! Stand, I say.

Midge   How now! And who are you, my friend? And who are these two with you?

Robin   Good Christian men, who like to help all travellers on their way.

Will Scarlet   I'll take your sack, good Miller.

Little John   And you can take a rest from work.

Midge   I give you thanks, but I am strong. I do not want your help.

Robin   Your sack looks heavy, friend. Perhaps it's full of silver and gold! I always say that gold is too heavy for a two-legged ass to carry.

Will Scarlet   Let's help him with his sack. ★

Midge   Put down my sack and let me go.

Little John   We'll not harm you, lad, if you hand over your sack like an honest man.

Midge   Do you know where you are? This is Robin Hood's land. Do you know what good Robin would do to you if he found you robbing an honest man like me?

Robin   I'm no more afraid of Robin Hood than I am of myself.

Little John   Now give up your money, Miller, before I rattle my stick about your ears.

Midge   No, no! Don't hit me. Truly I haven't a penny in my sack. It's only flour.

Little John   Is that so. We don't believe you. What's that at the bottom of the sack?

Will Scarlet   There's SOMETHING at the bottom of the sack.

Midge   Truly, there's only flour. I'll open up the top and you can all look right inside. Go on! Get your heads down. Look right inside. Look underneath the flour. And now take that . . . ★ and that . . . ★ and that! ★

Will Scarlet   Stop! Stop!

Little John   He's thrown the flour right in our eyes.

Will Scarlet   I can't see to find my stick.

Midge   You can feel mine upon your back instead. Take that . . . ★ and that . . . ★ and that! ★

Little John   Give over, Miller. We are your friends. This man is the Robin Hood you spoke of a little while ago.

Midge   Don't tell me lies. I'll give you all some more. Take that . . . ★ and that . . . ★ and that! ★

Robin   I'll show you that it's true. I'll blow my horn. ★

Little John   Now stand back there and you will see the greenwood come alive with Robin's band.

Midge   There must be twenty men all hiding in the trees.

Will Scarlet   They are all good Robin's men.

Robin   So put down you stick and let us know your name.

Midge   Alas! I am poor Midge, the Miller's Son.

Robin   You are the mightiest Midge my eyes have ever seen. Come! Will you join our band?

Midge   I'll do that gladly if you'll forget the blows I gave you all.

Robin   Then I have won the day and made a friend. Let us away to the greenwood tree and have a feast in honour of the mighty Midge. ★

And thus it was that Midge, the Miller's Son joined Robin Hood's band amid songs and feasting in the greenwood.

Chapter 3
Robin Hood and
Friar Tuck

Here are the people who take part in Chapter 3:
Robin Hood
Friar Tuck
Robin Hood is walking down the road. ★ *Suddenly he hears*
voices coming from the other side of the high bank. ★

Robin   That's strange! I can hear two men talking and yet their voices
sound the same. I'll take a look.
By my faith! There IS only one man and he's a man of God, a
Christian friar. He's the fattest friar I've ever seen and he's eating
a good, fat piece of pie.

Friar Tuck   Do I like pie?
Yes, I do like pie.

Robin   By my faith! He's talking to himself. I'll lie down here and watch.

Friar Tuck   Do I like wine?
Yes, I do like wine.

Robin   Ah! Now he'll take a drink of wine!

Friar Tuck Shall I take a drink of wine?
Yes, I'll take a drink of wine. ★

Robin I'll take him and his wine! I'll jump the bank and join him on the other side. One, two, three . . . ★

Friar Tuck How now! Who's this? Get back I say, or I'll . . .

Robin Put your sword away. I didn't come to fight, I came to drink. My throat is dry. I see you are a Christian friar, so you can't refuse an honest man a drink.

Friar Tuck I am too good a Christian friar to refuse any man a drink. So here you are. ★

Robin My thanks to you, good friar. ★ Do you know the countryside well round about here?

Friar Tuck I know it well.

Robin I'm looking for a certain man named Friar Tuck. Perhaps you know of him.

Friar Tuck Yes, I think I know the man.

Robin Then you can help me. Does he live on this side of the river or the other?

Friar Tuck I've heard it said he lives the other side. You'll have to cross the ford to find this friar.

Robin   I wear good clothes and do not wish to get them wet. You have broad shoulders, friar. Will you carry me across?

Friar Tuck   What! Me, a friar, carry you!

Robin   Didn't the good St Christopher carry a stranger across a river? You are a Christian man, so carry me.

Friar Tuck   By my soul, then I must do a Christian act and carry you.

Robin   Tuck up your robes to keep them dry. Bend down your back, good father, and take me on it. ★

Friar Tuck   Over we go . . . ★

Robin   Take care, good friar! The waters splash my clothes. It's deep here in the middle of the stream. Take care, I say! You'll have me off!

Friar Tuck   I'll have you off! ★ You'll make a mighty splash! ★ Ha, ha! I've got you off. And now I'm off! Ha, ha! ★

Robin   Stay! You villain! I'm coming after you. ★ I'll get you on the bank. ★ I'll carve you with my sword.

Friar Tuck	Come on and try! My sword is in my hand. Take that! ★
Robin	★ A Christian friar, with a sword beneath his robe! By my faith! This villain of a friar has got a coat of mail beneath his clothes. Right! Take that! ★
Friar Tuck	Left! Take that! ★
Robin	Up! Take that! ★
Friar Tuck	Down! Take that! ★
Robin	Go back! Take that, ★ and that! ★
Friar Tuck	Come here! Take that, ★ and that! ★
Robin	Stop! Hold your hand!
Friar Tuck	No! Let's fight on.
Robin	No, hold I say. We've not drawn blood.
Friar Tuck	I'll soon do that.
Robin	Hold! I ask a favour of you, friar.
Friar Tuck	Ask it, then we will fight again.
Robin	Just let me blow the whistle pipe that hangs about your neck. Then, to make it fair, I'll let you blow three times upon my horn. What do you say?

Friar Tuck   I say you are a fool! Ha, ha! Here, take it, fool, and blow. ★

Robin   Now take your turn upon my horn. ★ I'll get my own back now. Just watch between the trees.

Friar Tuck   I do! Here come my dogs. ★ They heard the whistle call. Get at him dogs! ★

Robin   By my faith! Four great hounds are bounding from the bushes. ★ I'll leap into this tree. ★ They must have answered the whistle's call, but ★ here come my men in Lincoln green. Shoot men! These dogs will have you by the throat. ★

Friar Tuck   At them, dogs! At them! ★

Robin   Why, what is this? ★ These dogs leap into the air and catch the arrows as they fly. ★

Friar Tuck   Down! Down, dogs! ★ Down, and come back here to me. ★

Robin   By my faith! What man is this whose dogs perform such wizard tricks?

Friar Tuck   I am no wizard, friend. I am the Friar Tuck whom you did seek.

Robin   And yet you never told me! I've had a ducking. I've spoilt my clothes and we've been fighting here an hour or more. Why didn't you tell me that you were Friar Tuck?

Friar Tuck   Because you didn't ask me, my young friend!

And thus it was that Robin Hood and Friar Tuck went back together to the greenwood tree in Sherwood.

Chapter 4
Robin Hood and the Lord Bishop of Nottingham

Here are the people who take part in Chapter 4:

Robin Hood

Little John

Will Scarlet

Midge, the Miller's Son

Friar Tuck

The Lord Bishop of Nottingham

Robin Hood is returning to the greenwood tree. ★ *Even at a distance he can see that his Merry Men are guarding the Lord Bishop of Nottingham, together with his horse and his treasure box.*

Will Scarlet   Stand back, Lord Bishop, our good master comes. ★

Robin   Ah! My Lord Bishop! I come with all speed, for I would rather see you here in the greenwood than any man in all England.

Bishop   Is this the way you and your thieving band treat a man as high and mighty in the land as the Lord Bishop of Nottingham?

Robin   I ask your Lordship's pardon if you have not been treated well. Which of my Merry Men was it who took you prisoner?

27

Bishop	This giant here, who stands full seven feet high. My friars took fright when they saw him and ran back into the forest out of sight.
Little John	I took him, Robin. I was the only one tall enough for such a high and mighty man as our Lord Bishop of Nottingham.
Bishop	And this young fellow here, who stands but five feet high, has called me vile names. So have these other men.
Midge	What did we call you, Bishop?
Bishop	You called me 'fat priest', 'man-eating bishop' and a great many more. And as for that mock priest of yours, he slapped me on the shoulder as though I were a pot-boy.
Friar Tuck	I am as good a priest as you, my Lord. As for the slap, it was a sign of friendship.
Robin	Did you call his Lordship a 'fat priest', Midge?
Midge	I must say that I did.
Robin	Which of you called him 'a man-eating bishop'?
Will Scarlet	I must say that I did.
Robin	Alas, that these things should be! For I have always found you truthful men!
Friar Tuck	Ha, ha! Ha, ha! We ARE truthful men, Robin! Ha, ha! Ha, ha! ★

Robin   I see our Lord Bishop's face is turning red. Stop your laughter, men.

Bishop   There must not be such laughter at a Bishop. The Sheriff will hear of this.

Robin   Forgive us, my Lord Bishop. We are not used to such high and mighty company. We are rough fellows, but not one of us will harm a hair of your Lordship's head.

Little John   We jest and laugh, my Lord, for here in the greenwood, we are all equal.

Will Scarlet   We are all MEN here, my Lord.

Midge   And all men are equal here.

Little John   There are no Sheriffs nor Barons nor Earls.

Friar Tuck   Nor Bishops, my Lord.

Robin   And so, my Lord Bishop, while you are here with us in the greenwood, you must share our life.

Bishop   It is your *food* that I would share.

Robin   And so you shall. This priest here is our cook. Come, Friar Tuck, bring forth the feast. Bring forth roast meats and red wine for our guest. ★

Little John   Sit down, Lord Bishop. Help yourself. ★

Friar Tuck   I'll be your pot-boy now. ★

Robin   By my faith! This is a goodly feast. Let the rattle of dishes join with the sound of talk and laughter. ★ Good cheer, my lads! ★

Merry Men   Good cheer to Robin Hood! ★

Little John   I see that you have feasted well, Lord Bishop.

Will Scarlet   And drunk our good, red wine.

Midge   Our wine is good and strong, my Lord.

Friar Tuck   There's nothing better than a good, *rich* wine. They tell me you are rich, Lord Bishop.

Little John   There are many who say that you are the richest Bishop in all England.

Bishop   The high and mighty of the land are never poor.

Friar Tuck   He says that he is rich.

Will Scarlet   That's good!

Midge   We welcome you, my Lord. We hope you'll come again.

Bishop   What do you mean?

Robin   We mean that you would not wish to leave this place without paying for your dinner. We'll take a just share of all you have, my Lord.

Bishop   What do you mean by 'all I have'?

Little John   We do not know how much you have, my Lord. I'll fetch the box and then we shall soon know. ★

Robin   It is a goodly box. Now, by my faith, you keep it locked. Why should that be?

Friar Tuck   Come Bishop, where's the key?

Bishop   I did not bring it with me.

Midge   Perhaps it's round your neck. I'll look and see.

Robin Hold, Midge! We must not lay a finger on his person. Go Will, and bring a sword. ★

Will Scarlet Here is the sword, good master.

Robin The box is strong and iron-bound, so strike it hard. ★

Midge The box still holds.

Friar Tuck Strike again, for it should open then. ★

Little John The clasp is gone. Come, lift the lid. ★ Oh, what a heap of gold!

Robin Hundreds of golden pounds! Little John! Will Scarlet! Count out the money. ★

Will Scarlet One hundred, two hundred, three hundred . . .

Little John . . . twelve hundred, thirteen hundred, fourteen hundred, FIFTEEN HUNDRED pounds in all.

Midge There's fifteen hundred pounds! Do we take all?

Little John The Bishop's rich. We'll take it all and share it out.

Bishop You thieves! You villains! The Sheriff shall hear of this!

Robin Hold back your threats, my Lord. We will not take it all. Now! One third of all this wealth shall be paid to us for your good entertainment. Another third shall go to charity and help the poor who live about these parts. Then this last third, you shall take back yourself, which is your right.

Bishop   My right! The money all belongs to me by right.

Little John   Let's put him on his horse and send him back to Nottingham with his five hundred pounds.

Will Scarlet   We'll set you free upon your horse, Lord Bishop.

Midge   We'll tie him to his horse and send him from the forest back to Nottingham.

Friar Tuck   Your horse will know the way, my Lord! ★

Bishop   I vow I'll make you sorry for this deed. The Sheriff will get you yet, you, Robin, and your thieving band.

And thus it was that the Bishop rode back to Nottingham, tied to his horse, and his box lighter by one thousand golden pounds.

Chapter 5
The Shooting Match

Here are the people who take part in Chapter 5:

Robin Hood
Little John
Will Scarlet
Midge, the Miller's Son
Friar Tuck

Robin Hood has just returned to Sherwood Forest. He blows three blasts on his horn, ★ and his Merry Men come running from the forest. ★

Will Scarlet   What news do you bring, good master?

Robin   News of good sport.

Midge   What sport, Robin? Tell us.

Robin   Our friend, the Sheriff of Nottingham, has called for a shooting match today.

Friar Tuck   What is the prize? Is it good ale, good wine, or a fine feast?

Robin	Not food, good friar. By my faith, you think of nothing else but food and drink. The prize is a golden arrow, given by the Sheriff.
Will Scarlet	That's a good prize, master.
Robin	Yes, Will, so good that it must be won by one of us. What do you say, men?
Merry Men	We'll go, Robin. We'll go.
Friar Tuck	Listen! ★ I hear footsteps.
Midge	★ Someone is running through the trees. It's Little John.

Little John	Robin! Robin! I have come straight from the Blue Boar Inn. I bring bad news. That rogue, the Sheriff, has set a trap for you.
Will Scarlet	A trap! Where?
Friar Tuck	Our Robin is too clever for the Sheriff's trap.
Midge	Besides, Robin's with us here, in the greenwood.
Robin	But not for long! I'm off to Nottingham to win the prize.
Little John	Good master, no! You must not go.
Robin	I go to win a golden arrow in a shooting match.
Little John	It is a trap to tempt you out of the forest so that you can be taken prisoner. I heard it all at the Blue Boar Inn. A price is on your head.
Friar Tuck	We will not let you go, good master.
Robin	None shall say that Robin is afraid.
Will Scarlet	Good master, do not go.
Midge	A price is on your head.
Robin	I shall not go as Robin Hood, my friends. There will be no sign of Lincoln green. My body will be clothed in scarlet rags. My beard and yellow hair I'll stain a walnut brown. One eye shall have a patch.

Friar Tuck   You see! Our Robin is too clever for the Sheriff's trap.

Robin   And you, my Merry Men, will go with me. You'll go as peasants, or as beggars clad in rags. In such disguise you'll stand aside and and watch. Away! ★

Merry Men   Away! To Nottingham! ★

✳   ✳   ✳

Little John   Will! Midge! Friar! Stay here, under cover, as our good master said. Be ready with your bows, but lie hidden under cover. I'll go forward alone and bring you news again. ★

Friar Tuck   Be careful, Little John. You're as tall as I am fat. Someone may notice you.

Will Scarlet   Look! There's our master. He's over by the Sheriff's tent.

Midge   There are six men standing ready to shoot. I can just see Robin in his red rags.

Friar Tuck   He stands out well in red. We shall see him wherever he is.

Will Scarlet   We can't hear much.

Midge   ★ Ah! Here's Little John come back.

Little John   All's well so far. Robin stands ready to shoot. The Sheriff little knows that the man who has a price upon his head stands but a few paces from him.

Friar Tuck Look! The archers have picked up their bows.

Little John I'll go back to my hiding place. ★ Stay here, in case you're needed.

Midge The first man shoots. ★ His arrow stands a finger from the target.

Will Scarlet And now the next. ★ Our Robin will shoot last. The next is close upon it . . . ★ and the next ★ . . . They cannot get it in . . . . ★

Friar Tuck The last one has. It stands right in the middle of the wood. Now it's Robin's turn . . . . ★

Midge By my faith! He's split the last man's arrow down the middle.

Will Scarlet His arrow wins the prize. It must! Our Robin wins!

Friar Tuck Tonight we'll have a greenwood feast. But listen! ★ I hear running feet.

Will Scarlet It's Little John.

Midge The greenwood trembles when you run, Little John.

Little John Our master's won the golden arrow. But when the prize was handed over, I saw an angry frown spread out upon the Sheriff's face.

Friar Tuck Why should that be? Our master won it fair and true.

Little John	Robin and he exchanged some words. There was an angry shout and Robin ran towards the gate. I'll not feel safe till our master's back with us.
Midge	He's coming now. ★ How now, Robin! Where's the prize?
Will Scarlet	Good master, you shot well.
Robin	Almost too well. The Sheriff wanted to make me an archer in his service.
Friar Tuck	What! Our Robin in the Sheriff's company!
Robin	He said, 'Say, good fellow, will you join my company?'
Will Scarlet	And what did you say, master?
Robin	Why, by my faith, I said, 'No man in all Merry England shall be my master.'
Midge	So he said? . . .
Robin	'Get you gone!' So here I am and here's the arrow that I won.
Little John	It is a goodly prize and won from the Sheriff's own hands.
Friar Tuck	I'll make a feast for this.
Robin	Wait, Friar! The feasting we'll delay an hour or two. I must let that Sheriff know who won the arrow from his hand. I heard him say, 'That coward Robin Hood dare not show his face here today.'

40

Will Scarlet   But how can you let him know, good master?

Robin   You'll take this scroll, tied to an arrow's head and shoot it through the window of the hall at Nottingham. Shoot straight among the dishes when the Sheriff's feasting in the hall.

Midge   What's written on the scroll?

Robin   It says: 'Now Heaven bless your grace this day,
Say all in sweet Sherwood,
For you did give the prize away
To merry Robin Hood.'

Little John   Fair words, Robin! This scroll will make the Sheriff's face turn red.

Robin   Begone, Will! Take care and join us for our feast tonight when we will celebrate. ★

And thus it was that Robin's message made the Sheriff mad with rage so that he swore to get revenge.

Chapter 6
The Rescue

Here are the people who take part in Chapter 6:
Robin Hood
Little John
Will Scarlet
Friar Tuck
Midge, the Miller's Son
The Sheriff of Nottingham
*Robin and his Merry Men are in hiding, because news has come
that the Sheriff's men are searching Sherwood Forest.*

Robin We've been hiding from the Sheriff's men for seven long days and nights. I'm getting restless for some sport. Which man among you can get to the Blue Boar Inn for news?

Little John I'll go.

Will Scarlet Let me.

Midge Let me go, master.

Friar Tuck I'll go, good Robin.

Robin   By my faith, you ARE a merry band! Friar, you're much too fat. They'll know you by your size! Midge is known because he's small and Little John is like a forest tree. So, Will, it must be you.

Will Scarlet   I'll go, good master.

Robin   Put on the Friar's gown, but hide your good broadsword beneath it. Find out what's going on and meet us tonight at six of the clock beneath the greenwood tree.

Robin   The forest's full of the Sheriff's men. Will Scarlet's two hours overdue. What can be keeping him?

Midge   Where's Little John?

Friar Tuck   Listen! Lie low. ★ Someone is running down the forest path.

Midge   It sounds like Little John.

Friar Tuck   It's him. ★ He's out of breath and panting hard. ★ Ho, Little
John! What news do you bring that makes you run so fast?

Little John   Will . . . Scarlet . . . has . . . been . . . taken. The Sheriff's men have
got him under lock and key in Nottingham town. Before I left the
Blue Boar Inn I heard it said, 'HE SHALL BE HANGED
TOMORROW DAY.'

Robin   By my faith! He shall NOT be hanged tomorrow day. Or if he is,
it shall be over my dead body.

Midge   And over mine.

Little John   We'll set him free!

Morry Mon   So say wo all. Wo'll cot him froo!

Robin   Tomorrow at dawn, we'll leave the forest here by separate paths,
then meet again in that same place from which you watched the
shooting match.

Midge   I know the place.

Friar Tuck   And I.

Little John   We'll meet together there and then we'll make our plan.

★   ★   ★

Midge   Here's Robin! Master! What's the news?

Robin   Will's to be hanged at noon.

Friar Tuck   Where, Robin, where?

Robin   Near the great gate of Nottingham town where the three roads meet. The Sheriff swears that Will shall die at noon as a warning to us all.

Little John   Will Scarlet shall never hang. We'll set him free.

Robin   Come men. We'll go to where the three roads meet beside the gate.

Midge   Is there a hiding place?

Robin   There is. The cover's good. They'll have Will in the prison cart. When it comes through the gate, we'll strike together through the men-at-arms and make him free. ★

★   ★   ★

Midge   Here comes the cart. ★

Little John   Will Scarlet's in it, guarded by six men-at-arms. You can leave the men-at-arms to me!

Friar Tuck   Leave one for me, Little John!

Robin   Keep back until I give the word. Now listen, men. I'll take the Sheriff and the fool who rides beside him. You, Little John, with Friar Tuck, will take the men-at-arms. You, Midge, leap on the cart and cut Will Scarlet's bonds. Once he's undone, we'll have another man to fight.

Little John   They're coming through the gate. ★

Robin NOW! ★

Sheriff Stand back, you villains!

Little John Stand back yourself! You and your men-at-arms! Take that! ★

Friar Tuck And that, ★ and that! ★

Sheriff This is the rebel Robin Hood! Take him, I tell you. Take him! ★

Little John Get to the cart. Get to Will Scarlet, Midge, and set him free. ★

Sheriff Stop them, you fools! ★

Robin No, good Sheriff, none of your men will stop us, nor will you. ★ See, I have your sword. Here, Will, take this! The Sheriff's lent his sword!

Will Scarlet I knew you'd come, good Robin. Give the Sheriff thanks. I need a sword. I'll take good care of it. Take that! ★

Sheriff Where are my men-at-arms? Strike back, you fools, and take these outlaws prisoner. ★

Robin Now three blasts on my horn, ★ for other help is near.

Little John Stand back! Stand back! The band of merry men whom you call outlaws, Sheriff, stand there between the trees. Listen! ★ Their arrows whistle round your head. Do you want them through your heart?

Sheriff	The outlaw band! Get back to town behind the wall, or we shall all be dead. ★ Get back, I say. ★
Robin	Hold, men! ★ Just send a bunch of arrows overhead to hurry them away. ★
Midge	Our Will is safe.
Friar Tuck	We're glad to have you back, Will Scarlet.
Will Scarlet	And glad I am to be amongst my friends once more. Thanks to you all. Thanks with all my heart.
Robin	Enough of talk. We must away. We'll move together under cover and back into the forest. There, under the greenwood tree, we'll have our talk and celebrate the safe return of good Will Scarlet. ★

And thus it was that Robin and his band rescued Will Scarlet and the Sheriff's anger grew.

Chapter 7
Robin hood tricks the Sheriff

Here are the people who take part in Chapter 7:
Robin Hood
Little John
Will Scarlet
Midge, the Miller's Son
Friar Tuck
The Sheriff of Nottingham
The Merry Men are talking together when they see a butcher coming towards them down the forest path. ★

Little John   Look! Here comes a butcher with a fine, new cart. ★ It's full of meat How is it that he comes this way and not towards Nottingham? ★

Friar Tuck   We need good meat. He's welcome here. Let's take a share, then send him on his way.

Midge   How now! I think I know that butcher's face.

Will Scarlet   Why! It's our good master Robin Hood, dressed in a butcher's clothes.

Little John   Welcome, master! You had us fooled. We were about to rob your
cart. But why are you dressed like this?

Friar Tuck   And how did you get this fine cart full of meat? It will make many
a good feast for us all.

Robin	No, Friar. This meat will not go down your throat. I have a plan. I vow I'll get even with that vile Sheriff who would have hanged our good Will Scarlet.
Will Scarlet	Tell us your plan, Robin.
Robin	I'm off to Nottingham with my butcher's cart. It's market day, when people from the countryside set up their stalls and sell their goods. I'll sell my meat so cheaply, that when the Sheriff hears of it, he'll come to buy.
Will Scarlet	Will you sell the meat cheaply to the Sheriff, master?
Friar Tuck	Not he! What mean you Robin? There's a trick in this.
Little John	The meat's not poisoned is it, master?
Robin	Heaven forbid! Why, no! When the good Sheriff comes to buy, I'll offer him the cattle on my farm for much less than they are worth.
Midge	What cattle, master?
Robin	The ones I haven't got! But if the Sheriff thinks he can buy cheaply, he'll come with me. And when we're near the forest's edge I'll . . .
Little John	. . . invite him to a forest feast!
Friar Tuck	Just like we did the Bishop.
Midge	We'll wait until we hear your call, good master.

Friar Tuck   The food is ready. All we need is Robin and the Sheriff.

Little John   Truly, it's time they had returned.

Midge   Good Robin will return, and when he does he'll bring the Sheriff with him.

Vill Scarlet   Listen! ★ A cart is coming over by the bridge.

Little John   I can hear voices. ★ One is Robin Hood's.

Midge   Look! Over there between the trees!

Vill Scarlet   It's Robin and the Sheriff.

Little John   The Sheriff's turned his head as if he's changed his mind.

Friar Tuck   But Robin's hand is on the bridle.

Midge   And there's Robin's horn. ★ Come on! ★

Vill Scarlet   What would you have, good master?

Robin   A goodly feast, for I have brought with me our good and worshipful master, the Sheriff of Nottingham, to dine with us tonight.

Sheriff   Let go my bridle, butcher. I'll not stay with you. This is the forest land where Robin Hood and all his thieving band do hide and carry out their wicked tricks.

Friar Tuck   My Lord Sheriff, don't you know this man whom you call 'butcher'?

Little John   The Robin Hood of whom you speak is that same butcher who brought you here.

Midge   And we are his Merry Men.

Will Scarlet   So sit you down and have a feast with us.

Friar Tuck   I am a better cook than any you will find in Nottingham, my Lord.

Robin   My Lord, we never send our friends back empty. Eat your fill.

Sheriff   I may as well, but by my faith, if I'm not back inside the town by sunset, all my men-at-arms will search for me. Take heed!

Midge   Take food, my Lord! ★

Will Scarlet   Take wine, my Lord! ★

Little John   Be of good cheer, my Lord. We do not harm our guests.

Friar Tuck   The meat you eat is the best in the land. ★

Midge   It came from your own deer.

Will Scarlet   It must be good.

Sheriff   I'll not stay here. I must go back to Nottingham.

Little John If you must go, then go you must. But haven't you forgotten something?

Sheriff Nothing at all. Nothing, I tell you.

Little John I say you have. This greenwood tree here is our inn, and in it you have feasted well. So you must pay your debt.

Merry Men Yes! Yes! You must pay your debt.

Sheriff Very well. I'll give you a few pence.

Robin You'll give us a few hundred pounds.

Sheriff I have no money.

Robin You brought three hundred pounds with you to buy my cattle, Lord Sheriff.

Will Scarlet Come, Sheriff, hand it over.

Midge And then we'll let you go.

Sheriff Take it then. But you and all your thieving band will pay for this. The King shall hear of what you've done today. You'll see!

Thus Robin Hood outwits the Sheriff once again.

Chapter 8
Robin Hood and King Richard

Here are the people who take part in Chapter 8:
Robin Hood
Little John
Will Scarlet
Midge, the Miller's Son
Frlar Tuck
King Richard (An unknown Abbot)
*King Richard, the Lionheart, is visiting Nottingham. Robin Hood
and his Merry Men are lying in wait for rich travellers to pass along
the road leading to the town.*

Little John   We should get good pickings today, lads, for it seems as if all the
world is travelling to Nottingham to see the King pass through.

Robin   Long live King Richard!

Merry Men   Long live the King!

Will Scarlet   I'd like to see the King myself.

Midge   We cannot go. The Sheriff's men are posted round the town.

Friar Tuck Ah! I would like to be there myself. There will be much feasting and drinking in the inns tonight.

Robin We are King Richard's loyal men whether we go to Nottingham or stay here in the forest. Our quarrel's with the Sheriff, not the King.

Little John Take cover, men! Some travellers are coming down the road. ★

Midge They're only friars, dressed in black, with nothing on their feet. They are poor Christian men.

Will Scarlet They'll have no money. We'll wait for something better.

Friar Tuck Not so! Their Abbot's with them.

Robin Some of these Christian friars are rich. Stay under cover, men. I'll take a closer look.
Hold, Master Abbot! ★

Abbot How now, fellow! Take back your hand from my horse's head. Can't you see we're holy men?

Robin By my faith! I know that all the holiness belonging to some high and mighty holy men could be dropped into a thimble.

Abbot You're quick with words, my friend. What is your name?

Robin They call me Robin Hood. Now does your heart begin to tremble, Master Abbot?

Abbot My heart beats well enough. So you're the Robin Hood they tell me of? Men hereabouts do say that you've been put outside the law for deeds against the King.

Robin You have not heard the truth. Our quarrel's with the Sheriff. My men and I are loyal to King Richard. But we're not here to talk. What money do you have?

Abbot Enough to buy some food and drink for honest Christian men, *from honest Christian men*.

Robin We'll treat you fairly. I'll call up my men. ★

Abbot By my faith! This is a goodly band. King Richard himself would be glad of such a goodly company.

Robin I'll tell you this, Master Abbot. There's not a man here who wouldn't pour out his blood like water for the King. What say you, men?

Merry Men Long live the King! Long live the King!

Little John Now will you dine with us tonight, good Master Abbot?

Abbot All my poor friars are in need of food and drink, but I'm not rich. What will it cost my purse?

Friar Tuck It matters little what you carry in your purse.

Will Scarlet We take our share.

Abbot What's that? What is your share?

Midge We take one half of what you have, whether it's pence or pounds.

Abbot I have one hundred pounds.

ill Scarlet So we'll have fifty from you.

Abbot It seems that all the tales I've heard of Robin Hood are true. You're honest thieves, if such a thing there is.

ittle John So honest that if you're man enough to fight with one of us, we hand the money back. BUT you must fight fair and WIN.

Abbot Well, Robin Hood, I owe you something for lifting the heavy weight of fifty pounds from my poor purse! I'll fight with YOU.

'ill Scarlet Good Abbot! Don't fight with Robin or you'll soon be down upon the ground.

Midge Fight ME, good Abbot, for you see I'm only small.

Friar Tuck Or me! I'm fat and slow to think and slow to move.

Abbot No! I'll tumble Robin Hood upon his ground under his greenwood tree.

Robin So be it. Take your stand.

Abbot If you have strength to stand, or breath inside your lungs in the next hour, I'll eat my crown! Take that! ★

Merry Men Look at that!

Little John   This is no gentle Abbot. His blow fell like a thunder bolt from heaven.

Robin   My head is buzzing as it was when Little John dropped me in the water by the bridge.

Will Scarlet   You've lost us fifty pounds, good master.

Midge   And got yourself a lump upon your head.

Friar Tuck   By my faith! I could serve this Abbot who can fell our Robin like a tree. I am a friar, Sir, and I can cook.

Robin   Stay! What was that you said? My head is swimming still, but, by my faith, I heard some talk of crowns.

Little John   So did we all. This Abbot swore to eat his crown. What does he mean?

Abbot   Turn back the Abbot's cowl from off my head, good Robin. Pull back the robe and you will see . . .

Merry Men   THE KING!

Robin   It's Richard, King of England! By my faith, I ask forgiveness for what's passed this day, your Majesty.

Richard   So the brave Robin kneels upon the ground with all his company.

Robin   We kneel before our King.

Merry Men   Long live the King! Long live the King!

Richard   I find you brave and loyal men of Richard, King of England. You are no longer outlaws from the land, but have your place inside my court. Arise, Sir Robin. Bid your men prepare a feast such as these greenwood trees have never seen before.

And thus it was that Richard, King of England, feasted in Sherwood Forest with Robin Hood and all his Merry Men.

can find out more about Robin Hood and his merry men by reading *Adventures of 'n Hood* (Puffin) and *The Merry Adventures of Robin Hood* by Howard Pyle (Dover)